Mosaics of Shadow and Light

✦

A Collection of Poetry and Prose

A. W. Jones

First Edition | 01
Paperback ISBN: 979-8-9885888-0-1

First Published | August 2023

Mosaics of Shadow and Light

✦

A Collection of Poetry and Prose

A. W. Jones

Table of Contents

The Dark Night of the Soul
Broken Hearts and Absent Gods
Sackcloth and Ashes
Band-Aids for Hemorrhages
Oceans of Silence
Wear a Crown
World on Fire
No Light
The Fertile Void
As Time Turns the Page
Blooming in the Dark
Starry Beginnings
Soul Retrieval
Sewing Yourself Back Together One Stitch at a Time
What the Glare Hides
Forever Hers
Promise
Acrostic Sunrise
Mosaics of Shadow and Light

Content Warning

This poetry collection acknowledges and addresses sensitive and potentially triggering topics, including complex childhood trauma, child abuse and neglect, parental substance abuse, intimate partner violence, mental illness and suicidal ideation, self-harm, eating disorders, religion and deconstruction, religious trauma, sexual assault, and death. Please exercise caution when reading this book. If you are struggling with any of the issues above or from anything not listed, please know that you are not alone, and help is available. You are loved, you are valued, and you are needed.

Suicide & Crisis Lifeline:
  988
  988lifeline.org

Substance Abuse and Mental Health Services Administration
  1-800-662-4357
  samhsa.gov

For those dancing through duality—through their own fragments of shadow and light—attempting to rediscover the remembrance of their wholeness.

INTRODUCTION |

"I am out with lanterns looking for myself."
— Emily Dickinson

Mosaics of Shadow and Light is the culmination of three years of writing and a lifetime of cycles of breaking and healing, repeatedly; a lifetime of lessons in healing by weaving together and unraveling the tapestry of my fragments of shadow and light.

Although poetry was a significant part of my personal expression (and survival) in my teen years, I had abandoned this aspect of myself for more scholarly endeavors. It wasn't until I was in graduate school and the life that I worked so hard to build began to fracture and fall apart all around me that I ran back to the safety of poetry to preserve any recognizable remnants of my life. But like all other times and cycles in life, I lost everything I tried to save, and the fight cost me my mental, emotional, physical, and spiritual health. I was left broken and alone, save for a few loved ones and poetry. *Mosaics of Shadow and Light* was born from the healing journey of arising from the ashes of my life, of being out with lanterns and looking for myself.

Although healing is not linear, this journey is divided into four parts for clarity. *Section One: fragments of cycle making and breaking* is about complex childhood trauma and the reparenting of my inner child to address my childhood wounds. *Section Two: fragments of hurt and healing,* documents my struggles with mental illness and surviving in a time and environment where mental illness was stigmatized as selfish and weak. *Section Three: fragments of love and loss* is about

v

love, heartbreak, life, and death. *Section Four: fragments of dark nights and resurrected dawns* is about religion, faith, deconstruction, spirituality, and feeling disconnected from the divine, and the darkness that comes with the painful dissolution of parts of ourselves that end up reawakening us to the truth of who we are and the love that we (unknowingly and knowingly) denied ourselves. It is about my crisis of faith and how a universe of more profound knowledge and spirituality opened up to embrace me as a result.

This collection is me, exposed in all of my brokenness and vulnerability and in all of my triumph and victory. It is a journey of healing through poetry and prose, a story from my perspective because it is the only story I know how to tell. My story is not inherently important; what is important is the space I hope you find within these words, for there is space waiting to hold you just as they held me in the darkest moments of existence when I felt the most invisible and alone. And there is space within these words waiting to buoy you up in the brightest moments of joy just as they uplifted me into sacred interconnectedness with everything all at once to finally glimpse what it is to feel infinite.

I hope you find the space waiting to be held for you, waiting to hold you through your own healing journey, your dance through your own fragments of shadow and light. I hope you find you, the exquisite and unique masterpiece that is you, and that you rediscover the remembrance of your own wholeness.

SECTION ONE

**fragments of cycle making
and breaking**

The Glass Child

A tiny strawberry-blonde with ice-blue eyes
and the fair skin of a dove.
You wear your fragile heart around your neck,
tied to a pastel-pink cord:
a perfume pendant of frosted glass
filled with liquid sunshine and arid desert winds,
waves of wild ocean air and rose-scented innocence.

Glass child,
too pure and delicate, too trusting and loving
to exist unbroken in this harsh world
tainted with antipathy, surrounded by apathy,
and filled with fear and loathing.
All weaponized to torment your sensitive soul,
mock your empathic heart,
and abuse your healing love.

Glass child,
those you love most stole your halo
and tore off your wings,
trying to make you less divine and them more holy.
They weren't successful with either,
but they never needed to be.
All that was needed was for you
to choke on words and suffocate on secrets,
starving that flame inside of you
until it flickered into embers
and cooled into ashes and smoke.

Glass child,
all that was needed was for your fragile heart
worn on that pastel-pink cord to tumble to the earth,
from your neck to the cement,
and explode into a million glittering splinters;
its rose-scented innocence
evaporating into the desert winds
and scorching sun.

Glass child,
left too broken to feel love,
but you never knew that feeling, anyway,
because you were never meant to.

You weren't there to be loved;
you were there because
you were a useful tool:
a little lantern shining pure and bright
enough to illuminate the darkness
and to divide it from the light,
a tiny filter that allowed the light to pass through,
a small receptacle with walls inside to contain the dark.
You never cared if all the pain you held
inside would break you,
but you cared enough to allow it to,
to try to prevent it from
breaking anyone else.

Glass child,
was there ever a time in your life
that you were whole or felt complete?
Or were you always fated to be broken
because you were never whole to begin with?

Mirror

Pure and pristine, a flawless
fragile figurine fractures into fragments;
a silhouette shattered, crushed by callous hands,
for you are without affection and hate your own blood,
and she is your mirror, reflecting back
a million little pieces of you.
You, where fear and darkness breed
seeds of abomination sown in antipathy,
that bloom into a harvest of animus and enmity,
choking the life out of everything
resembling innocence and forgiveness.
You, the creator of a scene deemed
too repulsive to view, one too revolting to admit to,
yet, the fingerprints engraved
onto the nails of the past
bear witness of your name
for all to see when her light shines upon them.
When her love for you feels the weight of your shame,
and to save you, she concludes
that she alone should carry all the blame.
A frightened little girl left to collect every splinter
with her slivered fingers, porcelain skin sliced open,
painted with crimson life and soaked in scarlet—
in an attempt to revive
all that once lived within her
that you felt compelled to kill
because it was dying in you.

Part I: Cycle Making

The eternal and abiding witness,
and unrelenting accompaniment,
ticks time down loudly into moments.
The same kind that flood into my mind
as memories stinging my eyes,
squeezing my chest in a grip so tight
the pressure makes it hard to breathe.
The vice meant to hold together
the shattering pieces of me
is the instrument now guilty
of crushing my heart and collapsing my lungs
until I've become a puddle of blood and tears
wishing to sink into the ground
and merge with layers of earth so deep
that I melt into Hell's molten core
and return to Pandora to lock within her box
my gifted portion of humanity's horror:
Every transgression and every sin,
every lie told and truth unspoken,
every mistake unforgiven,
every ignored supplication,
every scream and every cry,
every item weaponized,
every failed attempt to hide,
every vision of every demon
and of every not-so-dearly departed spirit
that torture you and haunt me.
The evil that you cannot see
inspires the evil that you will come to be,

both of which I will not escape.
Unholy plans unfold just as devised:
wars to rage throughout each night,
battles to compel the other to their knees
until the one wearing defeat is me.
And again, the cycle slowly repeats:
the evil that I can't unsee
is the evil that you've come to be
and one that I will not escape.
Lies birthed into reality
as the truth all would rather see.
Portrayals of vapid and fictitious scenes,
distortions of unholy alchemy.
Cast the guilty party as me,
now able to fulfill the need
to calm the craving for capitulation and victory,
in which another generation of parents
force a little child to shoulder all the blame.

The Reason Why

Bad. Stupid. Selfish. Evil. Me.
The reason why children are starving, why people are dying
continents away in countries I've never heard of but exist
because adults tell me they do, and I have to believe you about
everything because you've been to all the places that adults
talk about on the news and because you're an adult who
knows everything I don't, even where Africa is without a
globe. *Ungrateful me.* The reason why children are starving.

Because I'm four,
and I don't want to eat
strawberries with my pancakes.

Because I'm four,
and all I want is for you to stop yelling,
tall and terrifying, with your hands in my face.

Because I'm four,
and I'm crying because I'm afraid
because I'm not allowed to cry,
even when you're screaming at me
with your hands in my face,
and I just want to escape,
but I'm not allowed to leave the table
without being punished.

Because I'm four,
and all I want is to put on my black swimsuit,
the one with side ruffles and bright tropical flowers,

and fill my dirty white and blue plastic pool
with water from the garden hose
and pretend to be a mermaid.

Maybe Ariel because she looks like me
because I have blue eyes and long red hair
and want to be under the sea like her
or in my pool alone or anywhere but here.

Here, where Daddy's always angry and drunk by 9 am
and where Mommy's always sad but pretends
that nothing happens so she can forget
everything.

Because I'm four,
and all I want is to forget
that *I am the reason why*
everything bad exists.

Shame is a Daughter

From the moment I felt it—
The units of sound crawling up from my larynx
to be vomited out.

Something happened...

From the moment I opened my mouth—
The words spilling down my tongue and stumbling
past the cage of my teeth.

It was him...

From the moment I said it—
You were there to shove each word back down my throat
as a warning to never speak again
because good girls have closed legs and shut mouths.

Nothing happened!

As a warning to never speak again—
Because the next time, I just might choke on the secrets
and asphyxiate on the poison instead of idly holding
it in my stomach to be slowly eaten alive from the inside.

No one did anything!

Because in Women is the strength to take
men's unuttered confessions to the grave,
where they're laid to rest behind black eyelashes,
rose lipstick, and hushed whispers.

If he doesn't remember…

As another generation of girls prepares
to be thumbed through like the pages of a book—
dust jackets stripped, spines cracked to lay flat,
contents searched and then scavenged,
our corners folded—
bookmarking favorite places and passages
for quick retrieval, our highlights to be delivered
and devoured upon command.

If you don't remember…

Maybe that's why tradition
gifted education to the boys.
Because I am exactly what happens
when girls are allowed to learn too much,
so much that they forget to keep their mouths shut.
Because the moment I dared to open my mouth—
no one could stop me from saying
w h a t   h a p p e n e d   &   w h o   d i d   i t.

If no one remembers…

And maybe that's why after I told you
and from the moment you opened your mouth,
your purpose became to shut mine.

Because shame is a daughter
with an open mouth and who dares to speak
but not the uncle who pries apart her knees.

And guilty is she
who connects the dots between
the black holes of her memories
and has the audacity
to ask her mother for help
as she attempts to piece herself
and the truth back together.

It never happened!

And maybe that's why
from the moment you opened your mouth
I was wrong; you were right.
You defended yourself.
And you defended him.
You defended everyone.
But me.

Nothing ever happened
if you can't remember
everything!

And even though he is dead,
there's no relief when I still can't forget
or bring myself as an adult
to humble you with the truth.

Mom,
you were wrong
about everything.

The Uncomfortable Truth

A high tide of undercurrents
hides below the placid Pacific surface.
I'm screaming, sinking in black water,
pulled down by the undertow ever further,
helplessly drowning in nightmares of darkness.
Blinding light and spilled midnight ink,
fresh marks and blood spots—
judge my sanity by the shapes
that I make from the blots.
Pass out bottles and bottles of pills for me to take
in an attempt to correct
the imbalanced state of my brain;
unknown are their effects on my health and fate,
but overmedicating me will surely kill your pain.

So, don your black dress and adorn yourself with vanity;
pretend to mourn as you tally the score.
Paint yourself as the victim and heroine
in this modern, middle-class tragedy;
erase the proof and edit the truth
until you have everyone fooled.

Overflowing with venom and bitter composure,
eviscerate me with your verbal desecration;
castigate me for the weakness of my imperfection;
poison my demons until they no longer
mirror your reflection.
Erase the proof and edit the truth
because you have everyone fooled.

Eclipse me with the amber moon,
and let me paint upon its frozen glow:
scarlet roses, black violets, and tulips
the color of strawberry gashes.
Each a kiss and sentiment left by metal lips
and serpents' tongues on porcelain skin
painted pallid with a palette of ashes.
Asphyxiate me with your stolen halo;
suffocate me with my every dream,
rent into jagged fragments
and stuffed down my throat,
for the anoxic child cannot speak.
Erase the proof and edit the truth
because you have everyone fooled.

Thorns of pain rip into my side,
Tearing me apart, shredding my skin,
and serrating me into ribbons of worthless flesh
bearing bruises with your fingerprints.
Smash the cage that is my bones
and pretend they are pieces of the finest ivory.
Dig into me and unearth the infection of my emptiness,
excavate the space where my heart used to be,
manipulate my lungs to give me blood-eagle wings
so I can fly away to anywhere but home.

So, don your black dress and adorn yourself with vanity;
pretend to mourn as you tally the score.
Paint yourself as the victim and heroine
in this modern, middle-class tragedy,
where everyone places all the blame on me

and the starved, tortured boy in the body
of an alcoholic man already guilty
of similar crimes. Why would anyone have
cause to question or dare to raise an objection
when you already have everyone else fooled?

Yet when the tides of memories flood in
of a tiny strawberry blonde with ocean-blue eyes
running in terror in her footed pajamas:
her little legs struggling, her lungs burning,
and her tiny heart pounding and breaking.
Unable to hide from the sharp whacks of pain
indenting her cherubic face
and red welts blooming all over her body—
The shapes left behind were not
those from belts or switches,
the typical evidence assumed of men.
But they were the shapes leftover
from heavy hair brushes with stiff bristles
and those of wooden spoons and kitchen utensils.
Because the hearth is the heart of the home
and "the hand that rocks the cradle
is the hand that rules the world."

There is no need to erase the proof or edit the truth
when humans would rather choose to be fooled
by unquestioningly adhering to the notion
that forms of abuse
can be segregated by biology
instead of facing the uncomfortable truth—

that the most physically violent forms of abuse
a child could receive
could ever be
delivered by the hands of her mother.

Yet, here I am—
the inconvenient proof
of the uncomfortable truth
that you can never fool everyone.

Drunk on the Roof and Yelling at God

I found you drunk on the roof and yelling at God, and as the years pass, it's no longer a shock to watch you slowly poison yourself as you do and that somehow everything is still all my fault just for existing.

You're drunk on the roof and yelling at God, and I can't help but to add fuel to the fire, undeterred by the burn that may come from fanning the flames when they're all that I have to keep me warm, and when feeling pain is the only way that I know that I'm still alive.

You're drunk on the roof and yelling at God, but I can't hear anything above the booming echo of explosions that bloom from a flaming pit in the earth. Where alcohol streams and amber bottles gleam as each combusts into bursts of shrapnel and glittering fireworks. Shooting sparks and shards into the air of this star-spangled night that wears the red glare of war. Let shattering glass sing and let freedom ring because it's my Independence Day.

Because this is the last time:
I will be forcibly restrained to enable you to carve self-hatred into my heart, self-criticism into my mind, and self-loathing into my soul.

This is the last time:
I will only feel safe when you're gone; that fear will force me to sleep with a knife under my pillow.

This is the last time:
I will have to intercede and be forced to stand between you and the unbroken because no one else will and because I've already been damaged beyond repair.

This is the last time:
I will have to erase what remains of the evidence only to earn a brief reprieve of safety and from the shame of wearing the scent of your addiction on my skin.

This is the last time:
I will choke on my words when I'm expected to protect you, to be a good girl, to be a good daughter, and to escape the fate of what happens to bad children.

This is the last time:
I will suffer swallowing the truth to remain silent and bury your secrets only to find that your guilt was something that everyone already knew but did nothing about.

This is the last time:
You all will look into the eyes of a child and see their purity, testifying of a pain that she lacks the language to describe while being capable of absorbing every emotion.

This is the last time:
You'll be able to look into my eyes, sweet sixteen, mascara, and shades of suicide; a skeleton wearing the marks of self-loathing and self-harm, marred by the permanent scars of invisible abuse.

This is the last time:
You'll get away with knowing the truth and doing nothing while still being able to sleep soundly each night—when I never can. The last time that you'll avoid being haunted by the truth and still sleep comfortably through the night—when I never do.

This is the last time:
You'll be able to hide behind your middle-class dreams and white picket fence purchased through generations of sin victimizing the innocent. All existing as both the prey and the predator until the sacrifice born to pay the price does so in full to ensure that NO ONE will ever have to pay it again.

Because this is the last time this cycle repeats, the last time that after praying to God that I will wait for a miracle. This is the last time because it all ends with me.

This is the last time.
This is the last time.

No longer on the roof, you're passed out on the lawn; I don't know how you got down there, but I do know that I no longer care enough about anything anymore, let alone expending any calorie of energy in an attempt to answer that question.

Because I'm silently bleeding, shallowly breathing, and praying to God without making a sound, but why would volume matter when all my pleas were left unanswered? And when I'm uncertain if I'll even still be here by the time the fire trucks come to witness the miracle of a happily ever after.

But I made certain that when paramedics and police arrive, they will find where I've nailed your sins to the front of your white wooden gate, where I wrote my story in my own blood because no one believed me when it was told by the words of my mouth.

Do you believe me now?
Now that it doesn't matter?

My blood, the same medium used to mirror the words I painted along the entire length of your white picket fence. Because, dead or alive, you will find this type of evidence is not as easily erased as I am.

Though to the victim goes the fate of obscurity, increased is the certainty that the guilty will live in infamy, and my gift to you is this impeccably set scene for you to be crowned with this legacy in effortless flawlessness.

This will be the first time that the stain of your sins cannot be hidden or cleansed and that your sins will shout themselves from your rooftop for all to see. And everyone will until you're finally allowed to repaint that fence. Because, dead or alive, this is the first time you will not keep me silent.

The Sound of Silence

Screaming in silence,
the lump in my throat from a tongue severed traps words inside
of me. Suffocating, drowning me in emotions that aren't
allowed to exist but that I can't forget.
So, I don't make a sound.

Suffering in silence;
shivering in fear and in cowardice. Swallow them down, the
eruptions of acid ejected from the pit of my stomach, burning a
bitter taste in my mouth. Yet suppressing each gag damages less
than the torment when found.
So, I don't make a sound.

Hiding in silence,
suck in the emotions trying to pour out. Yet, solitary tears
trailing down the curves of my face can be found. Immediately
erase the evidence to prevent receiving something worth crying
about.
And don't make a sound.

Truth piercing the silence,
a life described in innocent rhymes: sticks and stones may break
my bones but leave too visible an injury; instead, you use words
to carve invisible scars into developing minds and onto tiny
hearts. Less incriminating but equally damaging, and with time
running out—
I don't make a sound.

Bearing the burden in silence:

the scarlet letter of shame and guardian of secrets that blood passes down. Sacrifice the one selected by the revolver in this Russian Roulette round. Play the role of defender standing between She Who Evades and She Who Lies in Wait. Chosen as tribute yet still in the frame of a child. She Who Protects always ensures that she is the only one found.
So, I make a sound.

We stare at each other in silence,
the rage pulsing through your veins collides with the love radiating from the depths of my spirit. To you I was given as flesh of your flesh; the combined halves of She Who Evades and He Who Fights: rainbow child and daughter of light—
She Who Protects and Endures without making a sound.

He sees in silence,
she who said, "send me," and was selected by Him to be sent to you as His gift. Instead, you defiled me by stealing my halo and tearing off my wings to make me less whole and you more holy. Yet, you succeeded at neither. Selling pearls of eternity for ashes of dreams, you attempt to erase the past to rewrite future endings, ignoring that destiny is created through editing the present. The Creator of creators witnesses all.
Both silent and sound.

The sound of forgiveness,
freely given from my healing soul, yet Mercy can't steal from Justice's lawful claim. My forgiveness cannot save you when vengeance is His, and pride denies my victimhood, your responsibility, and your heart from changing.

And at the Last Day, if you remain in denial of the childhood your abuse robbed and the pain that your neglect caused, and still cast upon me your blame; what I will say is Mercy can't steal from Justice's lawful claim—

If I'm asked to make a sound.

Hunger Pangs

Little One, please don't blame yourself
for believing the lies told to you by those you love.
By those who didn't love you
and those who never learned how to.
By those who said that you were never enough.
By those who taught you that you had to earn love
and that the price to be paid in exchange was perfection.
It isn't your fault for believing the same words
that so many have and will still fall for.
Because when you're left starving for love,
you'll eat anything to try to fill that hunger,
even when what others are serving
is so inferior to what you truly deserve.

Oceans (The Heavens Also Weep)

Little One, allow yourself to cry.
Emotions do not make you weak;
they are what make you human.
Your sensitivity is a gift,
and your empathy is a light
that shines in the dark.
Do not allow this harsh world
to turn you cold
and steal your softness
by snuffing out the sparks
that warm your heart
and set your soul on fire.
You were made to shine pure love,
a pillar of light for all to see
to show humanity a better way.
So, let your tears fall, Little One,
oceans of pain
condensed into tiny drops.
Know that you are not alone;
your angels will hold you as you cry
and wrap you in their wings.
They also know the pain that comes
from loving this world with such purity.
Because, like you, the Heavens weep;
their tears then gather to form the seas,
revealing the reason why each
crashing wave always tastes like salt.

Luminous

Little One, you radiate
with too pure a diamond light
to ever settle for being
a jewel in someone else's crown.

Your dignity and divinity
were never meant to be defined
by the lies of this world.

You are luminous with the ethereal glow
of love's indomitable flame,
one that can never be extinguished or tamed.
You are luminous even when
you and others cannot see you shine.

You, arrayed in robes of starlight.
You, adorned with crowns of constellations.
You, the enthroned Sovereign of your soul.

You are:
The cosmic dance of celestial magic,
the crowning glory of all creation,
the chosen vessel to carry the genesis of life,
the divine essence of pure love.

And inside of you lives:
Ancient wisdom, a sacred power,
an eternal destiny far greater
than any universe could contain.

Castles of Dreams

You grow among the
wildflowers, Little One.
Unlimited, untamed, unbound.
There has always been a part
of you that needs to be free.
To bloom in your own season,
vibrant velvet petals colored
according to your choosing.
Or to exchange being
an earth-bound beauty
for the chance to be a weed,
a dandelion dream
to be swept into the breeze
and dance upon the winds
as an unbridled wish.
To be carried to places
your eyes have never seen
and your mind never
could have envisioned:
realms of magic
and castles of dreams.
A place where sorrow, fear,
and pain no longer exists,
And a place where you can,
finally, feel safe.

Weaver of Worlds

Your tender heart is magic, Little One.
For some, it may be the only soft place in the world
where they can fall and feel the gentle warmth of love
envelop them as if they were wrapped in Angel wings.

You are the lighthouse, Little one,
ever beaming brightly into the storm,
drawing to you all who seek refuge
and the lost from every corner of the sea.

You are not only of this world, Little One.
You were formed from the universe—
veils of starlight and celestial dreams,
crystalline realms and sacred mysteries,
all wrapped within a mortal human skin.

Child of the Divine, pulse of the cosmic heart,
you are the rhythm of the universe dancing in motion:
the swirling of galaxies, the pivoting of planets,
the whirling of worlds, and portals through time
twirling together within the folds of your skirt.

With starlight in your eyes and healing in your hands,
spinning threads of magic out of chaos,
you weave together worlds too exalted for man.

Part II: Cycle Breaking

Though demonic plans unfold just as devised,
the dark can never hide from the light,
or steal from the Victor's prize,
all that He pronounces His.
Thus, He selected from among His children,
those called to be an instrument in His hand
and return to Him the heart of man:
sent to families with the task to break
cycles of sin and generations enslaved
in the captivity of the Evil One.
While from childhood's hour
being exposed to views of hell
that only the Savior and the serpent know:
the devil's domain that the Christ did overthrow.
Satan, in whatever guise, cannot hide
those who his eyes see as a prize;
he leaves his fingerprints upon their lives,
those who he tries to pry from the path of Light:
the future warriors, servants, and healers of Christ;
the highest threat to neutralize
whose end justifies the means.
Such is the story of my life.
In my weakness, I was chosen
by the Son of Man to accomplish
His work on the earth.
Strengthened by the hand of His might,
purified through His atoning sacrifice,
and to Him be all the glory given
that my generation will be the last to see and know

the evils I was tasked to overthrow.
My father's house now rests upon the rock of Christ,
He being chief Cornerstone;
with bloodlines, both past and future,
now joined and held in place
by a solitary keystone:
A child He sent in His name
to break the enemy's chains;
with Him, He knew that I would not fail.
Thus, before being born, He inspired
my mother to give me the name,
"beloved victory of the people."

SECTION TWO

**fragments of hurt
and healing**

Enfolding

Sometimes,
I wish I could be an angel
with feathery soft white wings.
Because having wings
means that I can wrap them
around myself like a hug
and hold myself to keep
the pieces of me in place
when I'm breaking apart,
and all I can do is cry
and gently rock myself
back and forth.
Alone.
Wings to take the place
of where another's arms
should be but have never been
or cared enough to go.
Wings that would care
when neither myself
nor others ever did.

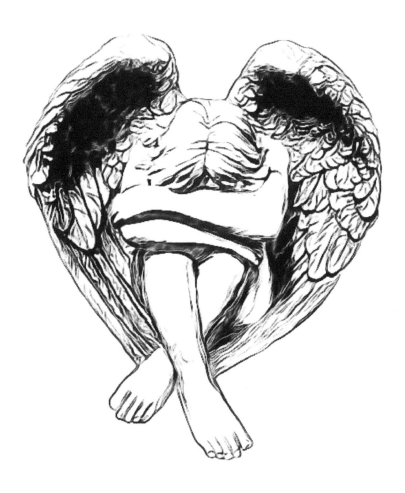

Where Rogue Dreams Go

The chance for renewal
dawning with another day.
Another attempt at
picking up my pieces,
the haunting reflections
of hypnotic visions
and idyllic wishes
that illuminate the ache
of bruised hearts
and reveal the chill
of glittering tears
freezing into stars,
permanent scars
burned into a forsaken sky.
One that has forgotten
the warmth that once
came from the sun,
as its glow fades
beyond distant horizons,
where rogue dreams go
when hope dies.

Anhedonia—

the hollow melancholy
filling the dark abyss
of existence,
collapsing and fragmenting
into nothingness.
Mirroring the uncharted expanse
of the human heart and mind,
the unexplored and unknown
reflecting the depth and breadth
of the ocean condensed
into a single droplet,
a solitary crystalline tear
traversing the curves of my face.
Absorbed into gravity's free fall,
crashing into the ground with a smash
and shattering like glass
into shards, splinters, and slivers.
The invisible shrapnel
buried like landmines
throughout the desolate
fields of my soul.
As I pray for the delivery
of the kindest of mercies,
that my next step forward
can be the one that brings
an end to everything.

Alice (I'm Numb to Everything but the Pain)

The music box plays that familiar song
as its tiny pink dancer twirls around and around.
Both keep performing on and on and on as
if propelled by the winding of an invisible hand.
The magic they fed me in childhood
left a bitter taste in my mouth,
a flavor revealing itself in another round
of the same poison I willingly swallow now.
While desperately praying that it might allow
me to escape from this very state
that my youth once imagined as freedom
and to return to a time when, as a child,
I once was innocent yet never whole.

My inner child drank the bottle that grew me tall,
and adult me swallowed the liquid to make me small.
Time is ticking down, yet the looking glass is still.
Both parts of me wait for Alice
because she knows which way to go
to find the cure that will make me feel nothing at all.

Fairytales should have never been so named.
Such a title conjures up images
of a bright-eyed innocence so sweet.
Like the colorful confections of
saccharine-laced sickness I once ate,
to which subsequent exposures to its illusions
conditioned such a strong aversion to its taste
that I would rather starve or eat lies.

But isn't that what fairytales are?

Children already know that good prevails
before fairytales teach them about evil.
And children already believe that castles
and kingdoms in magical realms
are where princes, princesses, heroes,
and fantastical beings dwell
before fairytales teach them that dragons can be killed
and that killing is one way that a prince becomes a hero.
And that the other way is by saving a princess
so beautiful that she can't help but endanger herself.
It is fairytales that teach children
that any woman who can string together
a coherent sentence and then dare to utter
it cannot be anything other than an evil witch.
A convenient invention for the hero-prince
who earns his prize by rescuing artificial femininity
and slaying marginalized womanhood
so that saving and slaying
make our prince a hero times two.

But children grow into adults addicted
to watching the news, despondent over
the "ever-sickening state of the world."
Desperately, they point fingers
at every opposing person and group
to nominate victims as villains,
and, from themselves,
wash away any claim to blame.
Wondering, "where is the world I once knew?"

Reminiscing fondly about the peace
and innocence of childhood,
fabricating a reality from the tales
chronicled in a storybook,
and willfully blinding their eyes
to remain ignorant of the truth—
that the world they once knew never left,
that the world we see now
is the echo of the stories from then.
Ideas ripped from a page
to be played out on a stage
written by unknown authors' pens.

So, I drank the bottle that grew me tall
and swallowed the liquid to make me small.
Time is ticking down, yet the looking glass is still.
Both parts of me wait for Alice
because she knows which way to go
to find the Cheshire Cat, whose grin is all aglow
to tell him that, sometimes, it matters less to know
where you are going than where you don't want to go.

And I drank every bottle,
but I'm still numb to everything but the pain.
But maybe, somewhere, there's a place
where I can feel alive again.
Time is running out,
and it only continues to tick down and down
as my vision grows too blurry to see
where that looking glass can be found.

All parts of me wait for Alice
because she knows which way to go
to follow the white rabbit down
underground into the tunnel of the rabbit hole
and query him for an answer
to that which he already knows,
about which road to take to make it
anywhere but home.

And from the blooming darkness,
my ears barely hear Alice say,
"Haste! We must haste, for he doesn't wait!"

Ruined Canvas

Whispers lamenting
bitter emptiness.
Nightmares invade
chaotic corridors
and traverse the abyss
of a fracturing mind.
Engulfed in distorted
illusions of hope and
languishing in existence.
Weaving scars of shadow
into unraveling sanity,
splintering sentience,
and slivers of solace
that slither within
fragile layers of skin.
Piercing violet veins
and blooming vibrant hues
of pigmented secrets
spilled upon alabaster views.
Painting the pleas
of a meaningless destiny
on the remnants of
a ruined canvas.

Colored Crimson (Girl Undone)

Dissociation,
disconnection
from mind and body.
Distorted reality,
merging and separating,
I'm a stranger inside
and outside of myself.

Suddenly yearning
for the softness of an embrace,
the magic of a warm touch
when fingertips trace
obscure shapes on my skin.

Embracing eternity
when forms blur,
illusions softly blooming,
invading memories
of lost promises now wither
in uninvited sorrow.

Insatiable gluttony,
a hidden hunger raging.
Silently waiting to devour
fragments of dark confessions
and faltering devotion
when bittersweet hesitation
melts into ravenous desire.

Seeking surrender
in vibrant wonder,
nightmares whisper
and visions linger
throughout the night
under the light
of the silver full moon.

The icy gloss of broken glass,
my fractured melancholy
softly falling and colored crimson,
as my trembling hands
futilely attempt to grasp
serrated shards of life,
the remnant puzzle pieces
of a girl undone.

The Art of Being Empty

Blueprints of loss and longing,
the architecture of hope and fear reflected
in the all-consuming construction perfected
within the art of being empty.

When all that glitters is golden emptiness
and within every tear is a sparkling diamond,
a jewel in the crown of hunger,
an offering of love so sharp and a pain soft
that it corrodes the skin and slices to the bone.

Enraptured enigma, ignominious ingenue,
the skeleton that your nightmares dreamed of
is the wish that the stars imploded to bring you
upon elliptic lullabies.

Arsenic-laced bones powder coated
with the glow
of selenite and rainbow moonstone.
Draped in black velvet graves
and despair decorated with delicate dahlias.

Monuments of bruised moments
and lacerations of false eyelashes,
oil eyes of ink-blotted abyss
and blood of decapitated roses
with love that drips like thorns.

Fragmented pigments of scarlet sin,
onyx darkness, and ivory lace.

You, a handcuffed psyche
worshiping the opalescent pangs
of cannibalistic euphoria,
feeding on the sprouted endings
from life imitating the art of being empty.

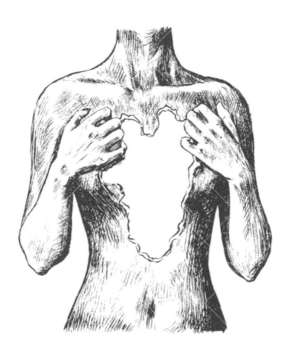

Lithium

The memory of your touch still lingers,
sending shockwaves of static through my skin,
and staining my porcelain with the warmth
of a sun-ripened apricot flush.
The slightest brush of your kiss,
your velvet winter slowly unfurling,
wraps itself around my limbs
and trails across my stomach,
setting fire to every inch of me;
awakening the primal creature within
that thirsts with breathless anticipation
for these secret moments of bliss
that follow the ecstatic agony
of recklessly attempting
to quench the insatiable desire
of the forbidden hunger
raging inside my bones.

You are my form of opium, my addiction:
the craving underlying my pleading,
the obsession compelling me to my knees,
crawling to a promise of an innocence tainted,
to my holy sanctum wearing
the remnants of your desecration.
Amplify the quickening of my capitulation
to seize the dull ache of bittersweet release
and the throbbing sting of sudden burning
that makes my numbness feel alive.

But I just want to stop...

Insidious in intent and pernicious in desire,
humanity preyed upon me in my weakness;
infiltrating my body and invading my organs,
engraving millennia of trauma onto my bones,
teaching me to hate myself while calling it love,
and the need to suffer violence to exorcise
from me the evil that I had become.

You are my form of lithium, my addiction,
a dangerous angel coated in stainless platinum;
an anesthetic cure toward a pathology rewired,
and one equally as calamitous as the pain it kills inside.
Wrapped in plastic safety,
you are the metal arms that embrace me;
the sharpness that soothes the itch of my every trigger
by leaving strawberry gashes sliced into my ivory skin.
With every razor blade kiss and bleeding caress,
you paint my pain in burgundy,
serenade my sins with scarlet,
and carve my confessions in crimson.

Because I just want to stop the hurting...

Self-injury, you are my addiction,
my bloody little secret that both cures me and kills me;
the relief that only finds me when I am cut open.

Because I just want to stop the hurting without hurting myself.

Chasing Ghosts

Inhaling—
The burning cold stings my insides
like slices from serrated knives,
as icicles form in my veins,
intricate crystalline grids of frozen lace
spreading and spiraling until I feel numb
to everything but the pain.

Exhaling—
My breath forms wisps of mist that float in the air,
life fleeing my lungs, hanging and fading,
until all meaning and time disappear,
leaving me clinging onto nothing
and having nothing left to lose.

Hollow—
Vacant and void; a desolation, bleak and bitter.
Forever a prisoner locked within a world
of eternal winter. Drowning in cold comfort,
the anesthetic that aids in concealing the ache
of scraping out my insides to keep you in,
of absorbing you into my skin,
locked away inside my cells
beyond the reach of any key.

Sorrow—
I keep holding onto the debris of decaying hope,
trying to breathe life back into dying memories
where the sound of your name stalks me
with the agony of silence and the anguish of your absence.

Because I don't know how to let you go,
and we both knew
that I would never be able to escape
and that I would likely never even try.

Solace—
The fear of rejection,
the familiar sound of derision,
your mocking laughter,
and acrid words from acidic tongues
echoing inside my disintegrating psyche
and splintering mind
bind me to the hope that you're still near.

Haunted—
I'll forever carry your ghost inside of me
if this final attempt makes you stay
because your presence and acceptance
hold the only hope that there may be
a remnant piece among the scattered shards of me
that is actually worth loving.

Abandoned—
In the mirror, my reflection appears
fragile and fractured, shrouded in surrender.
And in the silence, she whispers words
that echo inside my ears and slither inside me
only to escape by slipping through
pale and lifeless lips:

*I'm so tired of carrying the ghosts of people inside me
just to try to convince them to stay.*

Reviving Ophelia

Crystalline vessel, intricate and fragile,
a holy sanctuary for an immortal starlight soul.
A shelter for the flickering flame illuminating my heart,
the light in the darkness as I traverse the stars
and descend through dimensions into the unholy infinite
bound by the echoes of time.

Into a world where shadows fall,
and darkness follows into every place
where the hallows break.
Into a world wherein fragments of wishes
are whispered by a wandering soul
with missing wings and a stolen halo,
her fragile grace fracturing
like that of Ophelia, drowning in water,
crushed by the weight of others' sins.

Into a world where fiery hearts
are extinguished and their remnants scattered,
to witness the glow of dying embers
decorate the bitter wonderland of winter
in white snowflakes of ashes —
before being swallowed whole
by the hollow darkness after all hope is gone,
like an eternal eclipse of the sun:
withdrawing its light and warmth
from a species that killed its own home
because we lack mercy and hate our own blood.

Into a world where out of our shame,
we hide our eyes, wagering all of our hope on the lie
that by blocking our sight, we can continue to blind
ourselves from the truth of who and what we really are.
That by clenching our jaws and covering our lips,
we can rid ourselves from the ownership
of the crimes and sins that we commit.
As though erasing all proof or not speaking of truth
can placate Justice enough
to release fate from its proper sentence
or censor the truth within her verdict.

Into a world where we leave
all of our brokenness unmended,
ignoring that what we leave unhealed
becomes the brokenness that kills
the future's innocence.
Ignoring the silhouettes of secrets
that swirl around in the shadows of daylight
and the bouquets of fingerprints that bloom
into flowers colored in the vibrant hues of bruises,
as inconspicuous as spilled ink
and splattered pigments left to dry
and form blots of watercolor stains
on snowy paper and white marble floors.

Ignoring shards of ourselves sharp enough
to slice through layers of skin, yet unable to debride
our festering memories and infected dreams
or to sever the invisible ties that bind
immortal souls to their sickly human forms.

Ignoring shards of our brokenness sharp enough
to cut ourselves with our every attempt
to glue ourselves back together,
as we are judged for every mark or scar
earned from rescuing ourselves
or for any evidence of us ever being wounded
while winning the battle of staying alive,

Until we learn that wholeness doesn't matter now
if it ever did before, and alone we wonder
if we even matter when standing at life's crossroads,
debating if there is a difference between choosing
to walk down the road or to cross the street
when both are judged equally,
and neither path will bring you home again.

Because, in the end, it's you alone
who will be there when you hit rock bottom.
When you claw for solid ground
and the earth beneath you dissolves into sand.
When your fingers grow exhausted
from being unable to hold
what you clutch at and grasp.
When your bones are broken and aching
yet numb enough to escape
the joints of their past restraints.

Because, in the end, it's you alone
screaming and sinking in the silence of darkness:
hope fading and will failing as the world dissolves
into particles of crimson and black.

And after giving everything and receiving nothing,
you may finally understand why
all I want is to let go
of this crystalline vessel,
intricate and fragile, but a lead anchor
to my immortal starlight soul.
A soul who craves to carry hope
like how my body holds the ocean inside my lungs
as I float breathlessly in a shoreless sea,
weightless upon waves of mahogany melancholy
softly rocking me to sleep.

Call me Ophelia, for I am drowning in water,
crushed by the weight of others' sins
and without any hope of being revived.
And if I find myself too soon reawakened,
I pray that it be in an unknown place
that is anywhere but here—
any place that cannot hurt me
as much as this world and humanity did.

All That Remains

All that is above, mirrors that which is below;
what roots itself into the body,
claws chasmic holes into the soul.
Again, we drown in the abyss
of earthen walls dissolving into grains of existence
that slide like sand through useless hands,
unable to evade the gravity of time.

Eviscerated within the chrysalis,
we seek stasis and serenity within
nature's tomb of transformation
while hoping to escape the hallowed halls
of everything that is soul,
only to sew all that remains
of our hollow hearts and empty vessels
into the graveyards of the past.

Blooming decay and decomposition,
our disintegrating flesh
flakes into handfuls of dust.
Open your fist, blow, and make a wish
that any remnant of life will return
to flow once again below the skin.
To refill veins left to writhe and wither
like unrescued earthworms
slowly scorching in the summer sun
and tangling into knots of threads,
constricting breath and blood.
As all that remains attempts to slither
through parched tissues of riverbeds.

Collapsing and crumbling,
the debris of veins aimlessly
meandering and wandering
with no purpose but to wring
themselves out into shoreless seas:
satin droplets of liquid and iron
returning to salt and water
to paint visions of burgundy petals.
Dripping, diffusing, and blurring
into translucent ribbons of color
that slowly sink into endless saline.
Clear and cloudy, crystal and crimson.
All that remains culminating
into a climax of capitulation.

Ghost of a Memory

The winds of change blow the bitter
chill of winter through my hair.
Tresses that tangle into frozen flames
as the fire of autumn dissolves into embers
and sunsets of citrine, carnelian, and sapphire
fade into charcoal skies that converge
into solemn seas of gunmetal grief.

I shiver through mists of antimony
as the descending darkness swallows the sun,
bringing death to light and eternal night
to worlds of dreamland communion.
Through veils of petals and portals of moonlight,
I linger in the doorway of perpetual escape
to worlds unknown and of no return.

Worthy is my sacrifice and offering made
to pass through the galactic gateway
to all that we accept as forbidden.
A place where I am wrapped
in the ephemeral embrace of angel wings
and serenaded with the songs of Sirens.

A place where I am captivated by
the confounding collision of chaos and beauty
collapsing into the void of the blackest abyss,
how it mimics dilated pupils of pooled spilled ink
that drip into the letters of your name.
Hypnotic is the vision and bittersweet is the solace

found within the silhouettes of those syllables,
letters seared into my soul with scars gilded silver.
Forming lyrics strung together with starlight,
laced with whispers of burgundy wishes,
and bound by venomous threads of hollow vows
that flavor the poison within my glass vile.

A blend reminiscent of the apple of Eve
and the pomegranate of Hades.
The liquid comfort that withers my veins
into willowy webs of spindly tendrils
that feather into fissures that filter
life from a meaningless existence.
For I have danced with fate across
the threshold of permanent escape
From which there is no return.

So, wrap me in the ephemeral embrace of angel wings
and serenade me with the songs of Sirens.
Before my body returns to the dust,
and you plant forget-me-nots and black violets
next to my name, and I become another
ghost of a memory.

.

.

.

.

And regardless
of how much we love and give,
we'll always be too hard to remember
and too easily forgotten.

Night Flower

Like a night flower blooming,
I can feel myself opening
up to the darkness
to soak in the essence
of the night. The chemical elation
cascading from every sensation:
of every petal loosening,
separating and splitting,
vulnerably unfurling.
Each one, a unique expression
complete within itself.
Each one, a piece integral
to completing the whole—
of one night flower blooming.
A single note unfolding
within a midnight chorus
of a choir featuring
a species united in song.
Chords of melody and harmony,
each one revealing the mysteries
enclosed when enfolded.
Only to reopen, once again,
after the sky finishes
re-painting itself
as a black starry night
upon a canvas of darkness.

Dreams of Healing

The taking root of infinite dreams.
Their unfurling like glistening wings
fluttering within my soul
awakens the dormant within me
and thaws my heart back to life.
As the velvet night sky
yields to a crystalline sunrise,
a warmth once thought
forgotten caresses my skin.
And my ears open again
to Hope's morning duets
of melody and harmony
emanating from the trees.
Where perched on branches,
Freedom and Peace
joyfully sing the refrain
of their partner's song.

Times and Seasons

The critical degree.
The journey of self-mastery
over the past is now complete.
One cycle's end becomes
the genesis of new beginnings.
Of ignorance and innocence.
Of seeds not yet sprouting,
still buried in the dark.
Preparing for creation's spark
to ignite and catalyze
the sacred dance of life.
Of wholeness being broken,
a shell cracked open
to confront opposition
and learn from experience
what can only be gleaned
from weathering all of life's
times and seasons:
the agonizing misery
of shattered existence
and the resulting ecstasy
of overcoming everything.

Butterfly Eyes

Rainbows of refracted light
glittering in sequined skies
await to paint their iridescent hues
within your butterfly eyes,
the chrysalis-lined
windows to your soul.
Stenciled fragilely,
the flickering flame
and sparks of hope
that dare to defy the dark.
Metamorphic alchemy,
out of ashes and embers
arises a mosaic of shadow and light.
Cosmic dancer, star traveler,
the galaxies fluttering
in your wings
whisper remnants
of bejeweled lullabies,
ancient songs echoing
hauntingly harmonic melodies
that ripple throughout time.

To Ignite a Sacred Flame

I was always fated to be
consumed by the flames
and to wear its blaze
like butterfly wings.
To play with the fire unafraid,
even with the certainty
of being burned.
Fashioned with eyes to find
the beauty in every scar.
Because every mark
seared into my heart
also forged the keys
to undo each lock.
Freeing me from
the constraint of bonds
and finally allowing
my heart to beat uncaged.
Created to kindle
my own sparks of life,
to revive the magic
burning bright inside
with every attempt to
suffocate my fire.
And from the glowing embers
of my own smoldering coals,
I will take form,
and from my own ashes,
I will arise.

Reborn with healing in my wings
and my spirit singing:
the song of the heavens;
the chorus of the cosmos;
the echoes of eternal promise;
the sacred strain uniting
the past, present, and future.

The Lessons I Learned While Burning

I've walked tall through walls of flames
and have crawled through Hell
on hands and knees.
I am no longer afraid of the fire,
of the sharp and stabbing ache
that comes from being burned.
Because I have learned
from falling and from flying:
that what hurts us can also heal us;
that what decimates and destroys
can also purify and sanctify;
that what scars us with defeat
can also crown us with divinity;
that devastation is often
the genesis of healing and creation.
I have learned from the hurting
and the healing that wisdom
is only learning through experience.
Learning that we can form ourselves
into the remnant ash and ember of hellfire
or ignite ourselves into the pure
embodiment of eternal holy flames.
And that self-mastery is choosing
wisely which one to become
because the one we choose reflects
who and what we truly are.

fragments of love
and loss

Plaything

A plaything—
my heart tied to a string
and dragged across the ground
until dirty, ripped, and torn,
like a toddler's favorite blanket.
An attachment so normative,
that to it, a majority have been conditioned.
It's also, perhaps, the earliest
and the most subtle of examples—
that the more frayed and
shredded the remnants;
the more prolific the exhibited
patterns of devastation;
the more unrecognizable
and difficult it is to identify
the tattered remains of fabric
and debris of string as a blanket;
the more apt we are to label
the results of these
ever-increasing levels
of destruction as—

LOVE.
Even beloved or well-loved.

If we had the eyes to see
human hearts beyond our own,
I wonder how many would have
the same patterns of love

stitched into them,
like toddlers' favorite blankets
or playthings tied to strings,
dragged across the ground
until dirty, ripped, and torn;
so saturated with love that
they begin to disintegrate,
particle by particle,
until they disappear.

Why, then, are some
still unable to see
how and why some hearts
become trapped by love
when affection is blended
with dehumanization?
When we have been
conditioned to believe
that increasing amounts
of damage can coexist with
increasing amounts of love?

Hypnotized

Hypnotized by my light,
our polarities magnetized,
the gravity of my orbit
drew you in so close
that our trajectories crossed
and became intertwined.
Beguile and bind yourself
to the one who can provide
all that your soul insatiably craves
and that you innately despise,
the need for your darkness
to consume the light
and heal your shadow,
and the need for somewhere to hide
so that you can no longer
see your reflection.
And you don't know
if you'll ever stop falling.

Hypnotized by the depths
within your dark eyes,
I attempted to navigate
the uncharted oceans
between them and mine.
And by mistaking their shade
as the unfilled space inside
divots of damp earth
that nourishes all life,

the fertile ground of the soul
prepared to grow sown seeds of light,
I fell into the abyss of your eyes,
portals of black holes
swallowing light and flowing in time.
My surroundings ever-darken,
yet I still pour into you
all of the light of my soul.
And I don't know
if I'll ever stop falling.

Innocently unknowing
if we'll ever stop falling.

Innocently unknowing
because we were never taught how to love.

Innocently unknowing
if we were ever truly innocent.

Rabbit Holes to Wonderland

Your earthen eyes obscure a hidden abyss:
a portal of darkness without a hint
of what resides on the other side.
And I have always been too easily convinced
of a future with a purpose
when offered conditionally
by one with a silent heart and a loud mind,
with dark hair and an air of brooding melancholy.
One who excites every cell inside of me to scream
that you are the absolute worst of ideas.

Once upon a time, but no happily ever after.
The faulty heart of a guarded girl
and cautious daughter,
too prone to succumbing
to bouts of infatuation's insanity
and fits of hope's madness.
Endlessly searching for a sanctuary
of Elysian Fields of innocence.
One willing to house a timid gardener
who continually pulls
her roots out from the soil
while planting her heart everywhere
that love will not bloom.

Breadcrumb trails of nostalgia
scattered with broken promises.
Escape through the looking glass
and rabbit holes to wonderland.

Free-falling to the rock-bottom
of earthen walls dissolving
into particles of memories and regret
that slip through my hands,
unable to elude the abyss of dark eyes
or evade the erosion of time.

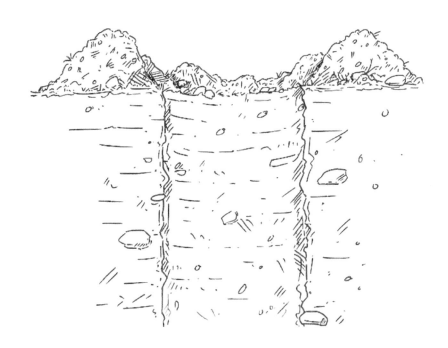

Where the Heart Is

If I close my eyes and imagine,
sometimes I believe, undoubtedly,
that I can hear you whisper softly to me,
 "Your heart is here, and here it will always be.
Please, come home."

And it hurts how much this is true,
with hundreds of miles of land between us.
Because every time that I return to you,
I always find a home to come back to,
a home that I never want to leave.

A home where I know, undoubtedly,
that I'll hear you whisper softly to me,
"Your heart is here, and here it will always be.
Please, don't go."

Tears from the Moon

Glowing opalescent droplets
of celestial sorrows fall.
Tears from the moon
traversing the waves of time
witness the unraveling
embroidery of our dreams
and the scattered ashes
of our memories,
emblazoned with scarlet
odes of melancholy
and sparks of severed sentiments
once shared that now
sculpt our mirrored scars,
as we whisper our
soliloquies of surrender
that paint the glittering
midnight sky in muted hues,
echoing the divergence
of our phoenix hearts
and crossed stars.

Words and Emotions

A myriad of words and emotions
swirl above me in wisps of mist,
weaving intricate patterns
of dreams and wishes
between stars that glitter and
shimmer like diamonds and pearls
stitched into the fabric of a black velvet sky.
I reach, and I grasp, but I can't seem to clasp
such elusive wonders with my hands:
those of dissolving clouds of hope
or the grains of the sands of time
slipping between my fingers.

And you left me standing there alone;
stranded in an ocean of haunted memories,
sinking deeper underwater with each crashing wave.
Having only icy salt water to dull the aching burn
of being branded with scarlet shame for an offense
so criminal it warranted a permanent reminder:
found guilty of being too difficult to love.

Wandering Hearts

Feminine mystique in the guise of promise,
birthed from the ascending dawn
and revealing siren-spun fire
woven into velvet lullabies jeweled with lies,
songs to soothe the soul and calm the mind.
While seductive spells hypnotize
in a subtle ploy to devour the now silent and blind.

Illusions uninvited,
fragmented visions of gilded memories entwine
with once vibrant dreams withered into nightmares
of yearning to fill this now empty space
where love's embrace once lingered.
The place where I first spied your face,
beguiled by your charm and
captivated by your enchanting eyes,
shining with shades of surrender and devotion
sacrificed to satisfy distortions of time.

Alabaster angel textured with petal-soft skin,
concealing magic sublime with veils of secrets.
Bury your light deep inside a heart made of ice:
swimming in seas of grief,
navigating waves of trauma and swells of scars
formed from the torrential downpours
of tears bitterly cried underneath silver moonlight.

Gathered hesitation echoes the faltering of pride.
Destiny descending, love's poison binds me to your side.

Pining for the soft touch of imaginary arms
while the sight of your smile fades to shadow.

Where do you go now that
my love is no longer enough for you?
Why do I stay and wait here,
idly, clinging onto counterfeit hope?
Alone and wondering why,
and consigned to conjecture
about to where or to whom
your wandering heart goes.

December

Awaken me when warm winters once again embrace California Decembers. When magic and wonder return to the season that once rekindled embers of hope within my soul. To a time when love's light could still pierce through unarmored muscle and flesh to melt the walls constraining my heart. When time would slowly peel away the layers of numbness within me, rebirthing the feeling of life and returning vitality to pulse through my thawing veins. *Take me back to any winter before you.*

Now, winter cuts through my skin to lodge itself within my chest, under the fragile cage of my bones, into a space where frigid winds can claim a home among the barren branches of my lungs and the feeble contractions of my heartbeat.

Now, every December has been reduced into fragments of fading daylight, shards of teardrops falling from blue eyes and bitter skies, and fracturing moments of holding too tightly onto memories that splinter into the ether—where only the ache of silence and the anguish of your absence remain.

Alone and left to wander the icy corridors of my mind, to chase echoes of hope and the ghosts of winter. The remnants of magic and wonder that I let your darkness hold, all that once sparked me back to life, disappeared with you and December. Leaving me with only cold winds to hold me as my hibernating heart freezes my body into a heavy sleep as I wait to be awoken by the warmth of the sun as it returns to me everything that you stole.

In My Arms

My arms will be the ones to hold you as you finally let go,
just as there have been others whom I've held there before.
And as each has slipped away
like grains of sand through my hands,
I've felt such profound gratitude knowing
that there is something beyond this mortal life.
Something beyond the way you now feel in my arms:
So thin, bones protruding, and cold skin tinged with blue.
Yet these are the times that I've found each of you
to be the most beautiful.

Though my arms grow heavy, and my heart waxes weary
as I cradle you and feel your life slowly fading,
I won't suffer you to endure this afraid and alone.
Despite how I will shatter hereafter,
I now hold myself together and

Refuse to break.

It's far more meaningful that my arms enfold you as you go,
so that love can be the final thing you see and feel and hear
of your time on earth as you journey to a place that far better
fits your worth than my lowly arms.
Until then, I will hold you to try to quiet the pain.
Within my embrace, I'll try to calm your suffering.
Until that bittersweet moment when you take your last breath,
and even though you're still resting in my arms,
You aren't here anymore.

And with gratitude,
I break
because I love you more
than you will ever know.

13:20 and 3 Hours Later

The heat of April is a treacherous betrayal now that ice is blooming inside my heart. The flowers unfurling their silk and unfolding their velvet in the brilliance of the sun, their pastel petaled salutations, are the cruelest mockery of the pain of death, of love's desire for the rain to drown everything set to bloom when their eyes are not here to behold the beauty of spring.

Because death for the living is swallowing knives that carve our insides to mirror our bleeding emptiness. Because love is pain when loss pulls veils between the realms over our eyes to obscure our vision while attempting to sever the ties that bind across times' distortions and dimensions.

Because my arms held you while you were still sewn into your body and during the blink that those threads disintegrated into light to carry you away into a world far more worthy for your sacredness to grace its grounds.

It's been nearly three hours, and though your body is no longer in sight, my mind can still picture you perfectly; I can still feel your forehead against my lips, and I swear I hear your footsteps in the hall.

It's been nearly three hours, and I am no longer holding you, but I am still wearing your death all over me. Though pain threatens to claw me open from the inside, and everyone insists it's best to strip this nightmare off me, the nightmare I fear the most is forgetting, and I would scour out my insides to hold you safely within me if I could. Because rinsing death from me means rinsing you from my skin, and I don't want to accept everything that comes with accepting that all of this is over.

Because all of this was over when you met peace at the very instant your soul slipped away. Because all of this is over for you even when it isn't over for me because your body is not yet in the ground.

Synchronicity of Loss

I buried you today, or what was left of you,
and as the moist earth covered your body,
I realized that the pain in death is for the living.
Because we give a piece of ourselves
to everyone we love, and them to us,
a part that never dies or recycles into the earth.
These mirrored images become puzzle pieces
to a hole in the soul that they alone can fit.

I buried you today, and I felt a piece of you
intertwine with my soul and swell with love inside me.
Like an ocean ever-rising with nowhere to flow
but to roll down my face and onto your grave,
while remembering the many times with you
that I sang our own version of "You are my Sunshine"
that's as true now as it was then:

"You are my sunshine, my only sunshine.
You make me happy all of my days.
You will never know how much I love you,
but you'll take a part of me with you,
to be beside you and remind you
that on your way home, my love will be with you,
to be the light to guide you on your way."

The Crossroads of Holding On and Letting Go

I wonder if it's warm where you are,
if you can feel the heat on your skin,
if your eyes can finally see the sun
that set here so long ago.
The only season I know now is winter.

I wonder if you feel less tired,
no longer wearing the weather inside your bones:
the numbingly bleak chill of hearts frozen to stone
and the bitter sting of humanity turned cold.
Yet, you always saw the divinity in everyone.

I wonder if your soul feels lighter,
no longer bearing the burden of carrying
everyone's darkness inside of your heart.
Fragile and strong like glass,
its fragmented shards refract
the rainbows of light you exchanged
to illuminate the way for all who wander or are lost.

I wonder if you can hear the birds sing
sweet melodies of freedom, harmonizing
with whispering winds and murmuring streams
and punctuated by the echoing crescendo of your laugh.
It's been so long since I've heard that sound;
I fear now that I wouldn't recognize it.

I wonder if you pick the wildflowers
and braid them into your hair.

I wonder which ones you would use
and the colors you'd choose.
I always saw you as the blending of hues:
the vibrant melting of red, orange, and pink
that the sun leaves as it sinks below the horizon
and diffuses into the softer pastels
of rose, violet, and blue
that color the view of twilight.

I wonder if there is night where you are
because you loved watching the stars.
Glittering sparks in the dark,
shining with the promise of hope.
I still survey the sky, hoping to find
the slightest glimpse of your light
now that you're far from here
in a place where there's no longer fear
or the ache of longing to be home.

I wonder if you can remember now
what happiness is, what wholeness feels like,
and the radiant joy that comes
when you finally feel loved.
I hope you can now be encircled by arms,
no longer fearing the harm
of what hurt their hands could do.

If so, I hope that someday you'll be able to tell me
if I can find a way to finally make it to where you are.

Ever-Unfolding Rose

Self-love is a seed already within you;
allow it to sink into your soul
and plant itself there.
Shelter it with tenderness.
Nurture it with sensitivity.
Nourish it with compassion.
Let it take root and bloom in patience,
to unfurl its beauty in the wisdom
of its own timing,
and you will find it to be
an ever-unfolding rose.

Healing Love

Let me peel away your pain with my hands
as you rest your weary head on my shoulder.
And if you need to cry, let me dry your eyes
as I hold you and kiss your every scar,
tasting the salt on your skin.

Let my love into your darkness
so that my light can shine,
reveal the beauty it hides,
and show you that every inch
of you is worth loving.

Let me sew together all that you call broken,
one stitch at a time, and embroider beauty
into the ugliness you see.
Luminous threads woven into iridescent webs
that glimmer with every shade of healing
so you may finally see the glow
that already radiates from you.

Let me shelter every fragile part of you
and be your protection
while you transform within your cocoon
until your journey from healing
to wholeness of self is complete.
And with strength renewed and newborn fortitude,
you can finally emerge from
the darkness of your tomb,
free at last from the bonds of the past.

And if once again
you begin to feel the dark night descend
and you fear succumbing to its shadow—

Let me be the lightning flash,
the electric spark that shocks
your dark stillness back to life.
And when the struggle ends,
and you feel once again
like you are whole and complete,
let me be the rolling thunder,
the echo of your heartbeat,
the gentle pulse rocking you to sleep
to face another tomorrow.

Éponine

Fragile flames flicker;
their movement, a familiar
hypnotic dance in the dark.
Liberating the subconscious,
releasing nightmares,
and engulfing your fears
in realms of shadow that bind you
to the black canvas of night.

Promises wither,
and melodies whisper
as love's once-gilded memories
collapse into mere moments
of inner hesitation
and internal reluctance,
states of suspension
and places of pause.
The pull of polarity,
positioned for division,
lingers in the liminal
and straddles the chasm
between my light and your shadow.

Let my love be a light of refuge
in your world of darkness.
A beacon to beckon you home
when you no longer feel
compelled to keep running
from all that frightens you.

Let my love be the candle
that envelops night's shadow
in the warmth of its soothing glow.
Give me your nightmares to keep,
and sleep in the reprieve of my dreams,
where my love will hold you in safety
while you sleep soundly
and give your weary soul rest.

Dreamers

Radiant dreamers of veiled mystery
and entwined destiny, together traversing
love's enigma of uncharted wonder,
gravity encompassing them
in the ecstasy of sweetest surrender.
Awakening a hidden hunger within them,
the yearning to explore heaven's
hypnotic visions of time's chains collapsing.
While engulfed in the aching desire that, together,
they can embrace the fire of the ascending sun.

Spiritual Flames

Inextricably intertwined.
Intricate webs of stars align,
forming glistening silver ties that bind
and weave through all dimensions of time,
embroidering orderly patterns into chaotic timelines
in realms where karma and fate collide
and destiny dances with the divine.

Finger to finger and palm to palm,
a locked gaze of star-laced eyes to wish upon.
Kindled sparks from before creation's dawn
ignite the sacred flame of love's immortal bond.
Elysian symphonies of celestial sonnets and psalms,
the refrain of the echoing heartbeat of the lovers' song.

Embracing entwined existence,
reminisce in memories of
the sweet smell of your skin.
Fragrant daydreams of velvet
rose petals kissing the wind,
gently falling to earthen floors
from cherubic hands of innocence.
Where the mirrored hearts of lovers
unite through eternal promises.
Perpetrating a cycle without
a beginning or end.

Eternal (Sirens and Stoics)

Unshackle me,
a prisoner of tangled emotions bound with lies,
a captive confined behind
walls of darkness cemented with secrets.
How I desperately dream of a daring deliverance
from the ghosts haunting the depths
of my subconscious abyss and to be free
from the incessant chase through the labyrinths
of chaotic corridors and cursed crossroads
to the crumbling cliffs that comprise my conscious mind.

Deliver me,
the prey ever praying for your arrival,
for your storm to be the terror
that tears down the fortress of my tower,
to uncaging me by demolishing rock into rubble
while leaving no stone unturned.
Release me by collapsing all of my defenses
and dissolving every layer of protection
that locks me out of the furnace of my heart.
Unleash every ounce of your destruction;
let the turmoil of your devastation rage.
I am not afraid of your weather,
no matter how volatile, for I was created
to withstand your every storm.

Cradle me,
an unworthy pilgrim, prone to stray and wander
from the safety of surrender
found in the tender embrace of your whisper.

I am a siren spellbound by the serene melody
of your voice softly singing to me
the lullabies I wrote for you in stolen starlight,
painted with the ashes of your nightmares
and the vibrant resurrection of your dreams,
and decorated with the glittering tears of the moon.

And then let me quiet your song
with a single touch,
the slightest grazing of my fingertips against your skin,
tracing my silent vows, written out letter by letter,
until my words sink through the walls of your chest
to bloom in the hollow halls of your heart.

Unravel me,
until I am undone,
an alabaster angel crowned with copper curls,
tangled and coiled around your fingers
as your hands gently cup my face.
Bathe me in the black silk of night:
cold rivers of fabric, fluid and flowing
over porcelain bones
draped in veils of pearlescent skin.

Shelter me,
engulfed in our velvet caress
of intertwined flesh against flesh,
and my heart will tell yours stories of a fire
that burns hotter than that of your demons
and one that shines so bright that your heart
will no longer desire the sun.

Even in Death

I planted your memory
in the unhealed shards of my heart.
There your love flourished and grew,
sprouting and sending forth roots,
knitting all of my brokenness together anew
with threads of a rainbow of colors
to match every shade of you.
Woven together, delicately embroidered,
and bound by knots of healing and love,
you mended my heart and restored it to life.
With your love blooming inside of me,
a part of you remains alive and will abide on earth,
enduring throughout time.
Because in every hand I hold,
in every tear cried upon my shoulder,
in every burden borne
to share the load carried by another,
and every feeble knee strengthened
by relieving another's grief:
there you will be, your love guiding mine
in my every deed of charity
and with those who follow after me.
I wonder if it disheartens those
who have departed from us to hear us
talk about love in past-tense,
as though it was subject to death:
that love simply dies when people do.
Love transcends mortality and time:

you'll live inside of my heart
for as long as your memory blooms.
Flowering gardens to testify
that your love endures
through the span of your life
and for all that remains of mine.

SECTION FOUR

fragments of dark nights
and resurrected dawns

The Dark Night of the Soul

It's the type of weary
that cuts you to the soul,
a heaviness within your bones
that crushes everything less dense.
It's the anchor that holds the ship in place
during the swells of the storm,
but you are tied to the same rope
and drowning in the ocean.
It's the burn of salty water invading
the delicate desert of your lungs
and the flash of white-hot lightning
incinerating its branches.
It's the hurricane itself
condensed into a solitary raindrop,
into a single tear falling from my eye
and dropping to the ground.
Someone told me once
that God counts the tears
of everyone who weeps
and that there will come a day
when He will sweep
all drops of sorrow from wet eyes
and dry damp faces.
But I've lived long enough to know
that I know nothing at all
and that it only takes a single second
or a solitary betrayal
to lose faith in everything,

for when a single promise is broken
or dream shattered,
or innocence violated,
it's easy to lose all belief
in anything sacred
that will keep any promises
at all.

Broken Hearts and Absent Gods

I roamed the lone wilderness alone, cried out to You lost in the desert, and sought You among the pavilions said to cover Your hiding place.

I have asked, but I have not received. I have searched, but I have not found. I have knocked, but I have not had any door or window opened up for me.

Still, I am convicted by Your admonitions that in my suffering, I am not yet as Job because I haven't yet lost everything, and I am left alone and wondering why my "not everything" does not matter to You when it is everything that matters to me.

I have only lost all that matters. I have only lost all that I have wanted. I have only lost all that I have worked for, all that You called just and good, all that You called my Path. And I have given You everything that I had in me to give, and I have sacrificed everything because You asked me to.

But in that very moment that I needed You to make up the difference so that I would not be pouring out my life into saltwater pools in the middle of the bathroom floor while trying to pick up the crumbling pieces of my existence alone for the hundredth time, in that very moment that I needed You to love me, that I needed You to show it because I needed to know that You loved and believed in me, to know that I was worth loving so that I could love myself...

At that very moment, You left me.

ALONE.

And what was left of me shattered into a million little pieces, glass teardrops glittering in the setting sun as the light faded and I descended into the darkness alone for the hundredth time.

Sackcloth and Ashes

In the darkest hour of my longest night,
In my moment of greatest need,
when I hit rock bottom at the wrong end of the tunnel,
and all of the light disappeared.
When I turned to my left and felt to my right,
and when all I heard after calling for you
was my voice screaming out Your name.
When my search for aid returned empty
and recited verses and hymns became hollow.
When all promises were left unfulfilled,
echoing in deafening silence.
When all meaning, belief, and hope,
like time slowly slipped away.
And when I was stranded, forgotten and forsaken,
and abandoned to fight alone.
After all of this time, all I want is to remind You:

Don't paint Your blame or wrath
in the form of guilt or shame upon me
as I emerge from the darkness after crawling
through Hell on my hands and knees
with the scars to prove it.
Not when all I needed was Someone to find me,
but I had to find the flame of my inner fire instead.
Don't paint jealousy or righteous anger upon me
when You can't endure my light because it isn't Yours.
Because of You, I had to become my own beacon,
my own city upon a hill that cannot be hidden.
Don't stretch out Your arm *now*,

now that Your conscience has reawakened
to the remembrance that I am engraved
upon Your palms.

You can't escape the sentence of Your condemnation
because You were the God who left me
in sackcloth and ashes.
From which,
I had to teach myself to rise as a Phoenix,
alone and on my own, for me and only me.
Because of You,
I had to become my own Goddess.

And since Your absence took nothing from my past,
Your presence won't add anything to my present and future.

And if You blame me, then my only response is this:

By abandoning me when I needed You the most, weren't
You the One teaching me how to live without You?

Band-Aids for Hemorrhages

Don't try to fix me after breaking me
to take credit for my learning
how to sew myself back together
one stitch at a time.
Not when all You did was hand me
band-aids for the hemorrhages
caused by You abandoning me,
leaving me to fight this war alone.
Battles that I never chose,
battles against Demons
that a girl has no chance of winning.
Battles where the price to be
paid for losing is my soul,
although I never consented
for it to be awarded as a prize
to the victor of Your
holy tug-of-war.

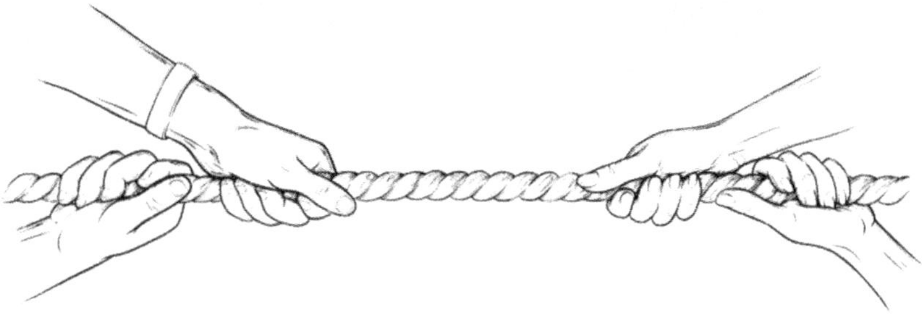

Oceans of Silence

Freedom—
     Liberation—
         And release.

I can see you standing there, crowned with glory, awe, and wonder, and surrounded by white light waves of peace. My clenched jaw and severed tongue subject my body to silence. While labeled forsaken, ejected from Heaven, you took my halo and tore off my wings.

Plummeting through the air, tumbling down to the earth.
     Faster. Faster. Faster. Too fast.

Flesh ripping, blood dripping from the wounds where my wings used to be freezing into droplets to be poured from the sky as I plunge into the ocean.

Darkness falls all around me, and the agonizing sting of saltwater invading my wounds burns my nerves until they no longer register pain. My body rises with each crest and falls with every cliff, a bobbing buoy of flesh, a floating speck carried to my silent grave upon the blackest waves under a graphite-colored sky.

Darkness falls all around me, and the piercing chill of deep water deflates my lungs, hypothermia silently making me numb, and I can no longer feel my chest expand to know if I am breathing or if my heart is still beating.

The dark night falls upon my soul; my body sinks in oceans of silence, and all I have for comfort is the echo of my voice screaming out your name, ricocheting off of every surrounding wave. And I pray to be saved one final time before going under, and the world around me fades to black.

Wear a Crown

Someday, I will wear a Crown.
Not one fashioned of silver and gold
or adorned with precious stones;
no feeling of shimmering cold
will imprint divinity into my skin.

Someday, I will wear a crown.
Not one of woven thorns as once was worn
by Him from ages long foretold,
the great I Am born to atone.
The price to be paid to right the score,
whose drops of blood from every pore
I'm unworthy to scrub from the earthen floor,
the worldly footstool of the Son.
Drawing to Him the souls He won,
the elect from before the earth was formed,
who from the crosses that they bore
now bear His name in reward.
Counting each lamb one by one,
the Shepherd knows all whom He calls His own.

But, nameless, I am left alone.
As sackcloth and ashes, I am shone
the beauty emanating from the glow
of the Jewels claimed by the Son
crowed-joint heirs in the Father's Kingdom.

Someday, I will wear a crown.
Not as a Jewel or child of renown,

with no room left for me in my Father's house.
But a daughter of the divine, I am,
and from these splintered hands, I can
fashion a crown of fault and deficiency
from the refuse, filth, and debris,
the remnants left over from creating me.
A broken body from the start,
too strong a spirit and too soft a heart
to endure a life of collecting scars,
a light that darkness tore apart.

I wiped tears from others' eyes
and succored the pain they held inside
while I was tormented by
the unworthiness of souls like mine.
Of souls like filters who divide
from black and white,
retain the shadow, and return the light.
Who build walls to lock the dark inside
for shame and guilt to hide behind.

Until the time that the evil one arrives,
though baptized in the name of Christ,
to attack during the Dark Night,
and with no one left on either side,
I continue to fight the good fight
until the light of life burns out inside.
Before the coming or appointed time,
no enduring to the end to justify
the terms of the contract for Eternal life.

Neither creditor satisfied
until Justice claims what Mercy denies,
my unworthy sacrifice and feeble attempt
to live a Christlike life for a Shepherd
to whom I am not recognized.

"Depart from me all ye unclean,"
though forsaken by my God unseen,
in my absent God, I still believe,
my faith and hope, a mustard seed.

So, for now, I wear this wire crown
with my tears like rain watering the ground,
nourishing this seed waiting to abound.
A future harvest from the years
that a girl and her wire crown
sowed the soil with tears.

World on Fire

Barren wilderness and forsaken desolation,
no nourishment remains to sustain my starving soil.
Nothing grows here anymore,
in the withering deprivation and destitution
of the degenerating wasteland of my soul.

Empty sun-scorched sky,
with nothing left to take flight
when melting wings are heavy
and when heavy things can't fly.
Because your shoulders already bear
the burden of the weight of the world.

Dreams dissolving into ashes
blur the sky like falling snow.
Innumerable as all of the grains of sand
in desert lands, where I've cried out to you
only to drink the water of my tears.

Silent darkness expands as the weary light resigns
for another night of purging every evil witnessed
that robs the light of its will to shine.
While the darkness can only mock
because the haunting atrocities
that the light does know
can only be viewed through the lens
of darkness's own shadow.

No Light

I've been locked underground, trapped and traversing the uncharted void of this abyss for so long that although Earth's hologram surrounds this expanse and my eyes can still discern the day from the night, the difference feels arbitrary, artificial, sterile—the stark anesthetic of a glacial white room where pallid feet weave steps throughout the labyrinth of a black sun.

The darkness of the darkest of dark nights is the weariness worn within the bones that everyone in the world could suffer simultaneously, and all could still feel alone.

And I feel alone and too inconsolably broken. Yet, my fragments are sloughing of skins of slivers, a shredded destruction still stabbing my fingers, the harrowing dissolution of an existence being sifted by time.

Yet, as before Paul was Saul, I knowingly kick myself against the pricks.

It feels like I've been crying myself my own oceans since birth and that saltwater swells have eroded my stone-carved walls, stripped me of layers of spiny shells and creaking floors, have drowned each version of me footed in false promises of love, and the pretense of survival, have baptized my every iteration in waves of change.

And since 2017, it feels like I've been crying myself a new globe of oceans, and I am still unsure if I will be able to wash these scales from my eyes or the darkness haunting my heart and mind.

Yet, my soul whispers in Phoenix tears and rose gold tones, "The darkness is a blessing and one that far too few experience because the anguish within its healing leaves the physician unappreciated, undervalued, and perpetually mis-understood."

And as the darkness expands, I feel the chasm within me fracture deeper, and I fall further.

Maybe there isn't light at the end of the tunnel. Maybe there isn't even a tunnel. Perhaps, it's a valley—my valley of the shadow of death, my vale of tears.

I think Rumi was right in stating that the wound is where the light enters you, but I think that this may only be part of the truth. Are we not souls of light born on this plane to learn about darkness, to experience it within ourselves, to learn more about light and love? Why would light need more light to enter the wound when it needs darkness to define it when it needs the darkness to shine? Perhaps, among other things, the wound is also where the darkness enters so that our inner light can be seen.

Because the light has been within all along, hiding like a frightened child because the darkness keeps trying to penetrate her locked barricade, as it floods in through every wound thick with its heaviness and excessive weight. Maybe, like a delicate flower, our inner light is waiting with a tremulous patience because all it knows is the shelter of fragility, and darkness is known for crushing all that is delicate and fragile. But it's this darkness that teaches the light what it is. It is the invasion of fear that teaches what love is not.

And as the darkness expands, I feel the chasm within me fracture deeper, and I fall further down into a cavernous expansion that feels like light floating upon molecules of peace.

Maybe the dawn is breaking and color is ready to repaint itself into the crystalline streams of a bleeding sunrise. Perhaps, the dawn is breaking, maybe I'm breaking, maybe both of us are, and maybe that makes all the difference.

Maybe May is the chaos that I've been recklessly attempting to evade and the chaos that my soul has been desperately craving to embrace.

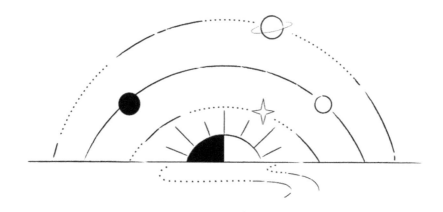

The Fertile Void

Agonizing is the pain,
and crippling the shame,
still being harrowed up
from the foundations of my soul.
My years lost in the dark night
have created the craving for
the glowing growth of sown
seeds of light. But for the new
to be planted and bloom,
the past must be pulled out
by its roots to break apart
the solid ground holding me
together and in place.
Because this soil is a space
that light needs to penetrate,
to illuminate the decay
and resurrect from the grave
everything haunted, unhealed,
and unholy that would siphon
life from new growth
and the potential rebirth of hope.
The miracle of the sun
repainting itself in the sky
to help bind up the brokenness
and find deliverance
from the ache of isolation
and freedom from this state
of suffering life alone.

As Time Turns the Page

All the words I left unsaid from life's best-laid plans that went
   awry,

Bloom anew from yesterday's ashes, resurrecting from hope's
   eternal springs—

Cocooning my chaotic resolve within a canvas of catharsis
   and a cacophony of confessions,

Detailing my dysmorphic delusions as they disintegrate into
   the deliverance of the velvet darkness,

Enfolding me within the ephemeral embrace of the effulgence
   emanating from Elysian Fields,

Formed from the alabaster sun melting into milky rivers that
   traverse iridescent pastel skies.

Grasping hope in my hands as dreams of healing flutter above
   me with promises glittering in their wings,

Hallowed light shines upon my empty vessel, the home to the
   voices echoing throughout the hollow halls of my heart,

Illuminating the incantations inscribed with inky pigments
   upon the fragile facade of my dry bones

Juxtaposed by odes of metallic gold and bejeweled notes and
   tones of watercolor filigree—

Keepsakes from the times of daisy dreams and dandelion
   wishes before thorns pricked my innocence to paint the
   roses red.

Lachrymose in lavender and copper waves of autumn, I linger
   within the lilac realms of liminal twilight

Mending my fractured melancholy with boughs of mahogany, enjoined by threads of silhouettes and strings of dreams—

Naiveté pirouettes in a floral print dress, wearing her perfume pendant heart around her neck with a pastel pink cord.

Obsequious angel perishing for love's promise of providing homes for the haunted within the folds of her soul,

Plunging her into the heart of the abyss, the fertile void of existence, a darkness so deep that it alchemizes into light—

Quaking light collides with the quivering of a chrysalis, its inner darkness yielding to opalescent oblivion as it unfolds,

Reflecting the radiance of rebirth and the luminous emergence of new beginnings

Surfacing from the bittersweet solace of surrendering to and surviving all suffering and struggle

To triumphantly witness the carnelian sunrise bursting through the night, pulsing through the glistening tissue mosaics of your wings.

Undulating, unfolding, unfurling in the chaotic serenity of synchrony and serendipity;

Voluminous and vibrant in velvet victory and blood-orange majesty, a Monarch feasting on the nectar of royal-colored flowers.

Wings of dandelion wishes, wings of glittering promises fulfilled, wings of healing dreams, where

Xanthic pollen suns rise from the graveyards of the past to be crowned with snowy petals of innocence, and

Years of yesterdays, of blood and pain, are consumed in ash, washed away, and replaced by thornless roses that only bloom in ivory, as

Zeal for life reappears with the return of spring, and past regrets of plans upset and words unsaid are left to disappear with the last of the winter's winds.

Blooming in the Dark

The journey is always dark in the beginning
when you are first awakening,
just as the butterfly's beginning
is not the light outside the chrysalis
but the darkness within.
Like the metamorphosis of the caterpillar,
you are blooming in the dark
and will emerge after the struggle
from the darkness into light.
Wearing rainbows of iridescence
and kaleidoscopes of color,
a glittering mosaic
of every battle
overcome.

Starry Beginnings

Spiritual alchemy,
succumbing to the shadow
yields to lessons in light.
Like a flower blooming,
petals unfurling one by one,
your fracturing is only the feeling
of vulnerability from opening
yourself up to transformation
to reawaken through transmutation
to the remembrance of your wholeness:
you will never break,
and you were never broken.
Child of the cosmos, you are
navigating the journey
back to remembering
the story of your soul.
Dare to traverse the uncharted universe:
to enter into dimensions unknown,
to sail through seas of swirling light
only to be swallowed by
churning tunnels of darkness.
Because even black holes
can birth starry beginnings.

Soul Retrieval

Fractured and fragmented,
portions of soul lost to
dimensions of space and time.
Lingering in the liminal,
walking between the worlds,
calling all that is eternal
to return home through
the sacred portal of your heart.
Wherein lies the secret
to the ancient alchemy of healing:
reintegrating the retrieved,
reweaving divinity into the infinite,
and reawakening the dormant
to heal your soul into wholeness.
Coming full circle to the
revelation of existence:
the state of inseparable oneness
between the outer universe
and the one beneath your skin.

Reflections on Healing

Gaia is a school,
and we're all here to learn
how to grow and how to heal.
Here to learn that, sometimes,
growing and healing look like
being huddled on the ground,
cradling your head in the space between
your arms hugging your knees.
Swaying to and fro, rocking back and forth,
until the imbalanced loses balance
and falls with a thud to rattle and to roll
in the fetal position on the unforgiving floor.
Where the construct of time is suspended
in the light of night or the dark of day,
where tomorrow always comes
in the guise of today, when you're already
numb to everything but the pain
that always feels the same
in a world forever changing
into an even more alien place -
until the planet feels dead to you,
but you both are still so fully
and unforgettably alive.
Where seconds are grains in wood
or fibers in carpet or microscopic pores
on the polished tile floor that bleed and blur
into uncountable forms that bear witness
of a temporary human experience.
Of learning. Of growing. Of healing.

Sewing Yourself Back Together One Stitch at a Time

Healing is the journey of the self returning to the sacred essence of the soul through transcending the veils of forgetfulness and illusion and remembering our wholeness and divinity through our earthly experience of simultaneously being both the wounded and the healer.

And as the wounded, I have learned that some of our most beautiful scars come from being broken and slowly sewing ourselves back together one stitch at a time. Using threads of 1000 colors to embroider delicately petaled patterns of love, mercy, and forgiveness onto the ever-flowing tapestry of the eternal soul.

As the wounded, I have learned that some of our most beautiful scars are formed from darkness by the knitting together threads of black webs into intricate knots of macramé. Creating fabric frames to hold in place the fragile geometric shapes of the fractured window panes of our souls. With glass stained in joy's spectrum of tangerine-orange hues and shattered by stones that the broken did throw.

As the healer, I have learned that every scar confirms that you are the magic of the magician and the transmutation of the alchemist. For with nothing but string and a broken kaleidoscope, you fashioned the sunrise into gleaming wisps of wings with a brilliant iridescence and fiery radiance that all of nature envies. Reminiscent of those of the Monarch butterfly, who, in breathtaking swarms, take their flight to reign over the skies.

As the wounded and the healer, I have learned that our most beautiful scars are healed with love. Ignoring the derision and mockery of the wounded who broke you because they are envious of the power or threatened by the strength of one who can pick up every fragment of themselves with dignity and will their broken self whole through the revolution of self-love while loving others through the miracle of forgiveness. Fueled by the same flame of divinity that shines so brightly within each of us to help us bring healing to our shadow and to thaw our too easily frozen hearts: an experience often too agonizing in both fear and pain that many chose to bury that same divine fire burning within themselves so long ago.

What the Glare Hides

Beyond robotic minds and mechanical eyes,
below the cacophony of whispered confessions
revealed in riddles of lies,
you'll find the secret of what the glare hides
behind wisps of smoke intertwined
and the tremulous glow of quaking light.

Where out of decay and from ashes arise
the soul's immortal coals to ignite a fire inside.
A torch burning bright,
its flame raised toward the sky,
illuminates a fate unknown and destiny undefined.

Blank sheets filling volumes
of unwritten rhetoric and rhyme.
The poet's pen silenced by
the blank slate of the mind.
Language confined to the abyss
between human hearts and minds.
Fabricated forgetfulness that dissolves
meaning over time.

Wandering the liminal where worlds divide
to find remnant aspects of self left behind.
Missing slivers of life, like puzzle pieces cast aside,
and portions of the soul fractured in time.

Coming full circle once again by design,
creation's balance to strike

and shards of self to align.
Each turn of the kaleidoscope
assigns how the fragments combine.
A rainbow mosaic of shadow and light
forming a portrait of Heaven sublime:
the masterpiece of divinity actualized.

Forever Hers

The Son,
born to take upon Himself the spirit of the Sun,
the light that shines in the darkness,
that set below all things to rise above all things,
He who overcame the world and transformed
her with His blood,
bestowing upon her a new form of transmutation
selflessly made available to us all.

According to my memory of this plane of existence,
You were the first to call me a goddess.
You, the Master of all ascended masters,
creator of the way to eternal life;
You, the mouthpiece of Father,
calling me a high priestess.
Your Holiness never took offense that my spirit
always thirsted for more,
knowing there was more,
that there existed divinity that looked like me,
an archetype of Holy Femininity,
the counterpart to the Father
that we call Mother.

I ached for Her in my blood and hungered
for Her in my bones,
a craving for connection beyond all I had ever felt before.
And although I've been taught time and time again
that You and the Father should be enough,

You never denied me the opportunity
to seek after Her love,
and in the same way that I am forever Yours,
in the flesh, I now also get to be forever Hers.

Promise

Serene aching, relieved
in cathartic reverie.
The promise of a violent healing
from a benevolent breaking.
The soul's dark night collapsing,
resurrecting a glowing dawn
rising from the ashes of a burning sky
blooming in radiant wonder,
enlightening the obfuscated
and birthing whispers
of breathtaking surrender.
Gleaming teardrops
weave kaleidoscopes
of crystalline veils
as effulgence emanates
from opalescent dreams,
cocooning me in the
promise of tomorrow.

Acrostic Sunrise

Silently, the starry night yields to the glory of the dawn's
   sublime, effulgent rays of light,

Unfurling petals of vibrant blood-orange hues and blooming
   jewels of shimmering gold.

New hope springs to flight, replacing dreamtime lullabies
   with symphonies of harmonic melodies,

Reawakening dormant life with a cacophony of song as the
   sky ignites into a wildfire burning,

Intermingling shades of flames with the resplendent brilliance
   of illumination ever brightening,

Spanning from horizon to horizon as the burning dawn
   surrenders to bright daylight.

Encircled in the transcendent cycle of life: a story of beauty
   so breathtaking that it could only be authored by the
   divine.

Mosaics of Shadow and Light

I am finding myself in the darkness.
I am finding myself in the light.
Glittering fragments of wholeness:
a mosaic of every self
that I have been and have yet to be.
Though I am still arranging my pieces,
I am finally becoming
who I have always wanted to be:
a version of me—
a handcrafted masterpiece
of breaking and healing—
that I can wholeheartedly
L O V E
in my shadow and in my light.

EPILOGUE |

Lessons from Liminal Forces of Nature

I can feel myself changing, flowing with the current of my inner knowing, as all within and without mirror the same shifting of the seasons of life. I can feel myself changing, finally floating to the surface, emerging from the darkness that my inner sun has pushed outward, upward, and onward.

Healing isn't always cracking open, rooting yourself, and blooming where you are planted. Sometimes, it is dredging up the ocean floor until you find the light—the flaming fire—that doesn't go out in dark water or in the hemorrhaging of spiritual blood being harrowed up from the foundation of your soul.

Healing isn't always waking up from the darkness to light streaking toward your eyes from a bleeding sunrise. Sometimes, healing is the inner knowing that your time in the darkness is over, and the only thing preventing you from picking up your torch and walking toward the light is you making that choice. And I finally feel able and worthy to choose that for myself.

The time of being out with lanterns and looking for myself is coming to an end, for I have found her holding a torch of fire, preparing a new story to tell.

To be continued...

NOTES |

- The necklace pictured in *The Glass Child*, the Heart Drops Cologne Pendant from Avon, is the necklace I had as a child that shattered on impact with the cement after it slipped through my fingers while trying to twist the glass heart back into its golden cap.

- *Mirror* and *Reviving Ophelia* both reference the line "...for they are without affection and hate their own blood." from *The Pearl of Great Price*. In addition, *Mirror* was influenced by Jewel's *Pieces of You*.

- *The Reason Why* is a poem based on an actual experience of my picky childhood eating. Verbal abuse was a constant throughout my childhood and adolescence.

- *Shame is a Daughter* is based on the psychological fallout of a conversation of this nature I had with my mother as an adult about "an incident" in childhood.

- In *The Uncomfortable Truth*, the line, "the hand that rocks the cradle is the hand that rules the world," comes from William Ross Wallace's poem *The Hand that Rocks the Cradle is the Hand that Rules the World*.

- *Drunk on the Roof and Yelling at God*, though based on my father's alcoholism, is not based on actual events but was inspired by Martina McBride's song *Independence Day*. My father's alcoholism was a constant throughout my childhood and adolescence.

- The poems that mention "Little One" are my inner child healing and reparenting poems. I have found this technique to be a powerful way to help me heal childhood wounds.

- *Part II: Cycle Breaking*, although this poem may come across as somewhat egoist, it's about the role of cycle-breaker and my feeling of being "sent here" to take this role upon myself, which started at an extremely young age. It's a motivational poem that has helped me to stay strong during dark and painful times. Also, the line about being named "beloved victory of the people" refers specifically to the meanings of my first and middle names and is not an explicit reference as to how I see or feel about myself.

- The poems *Alice (Numb to Everything but the Pain)* and *Rabbit Holes to Wonderland* reference Lewis Carroll's *Alice's Adventures in Wonderland and Through the Looking Glass*.

- *The Art of Being Empty* is about my struggles with anorexia while growing up and my continuing struggles with body dysmorphia as an adult. If you are struggling with this, please consider seeking help from qualified and trusted medical and/or psychological professionals.

- *Lithium* is about my struggle with self-harm and its use as a coping mechanism. Not all self-harm is engaged in with the purpose of suicide. If you are struggling with this, please consider seeking help from qualified and trusted medical and/or psychological professionals.

+ The poem *Reviving Ophelia* references the character of Ophelia from William Shakespeare's *Hamlet*, who drowns after descending into madness from her father's murder. The poem's title comes from the book *Reviving Ophelia: Saving the Selves of Adolescent Girls* by Mary Pipher, Ph.D., and was influenced by Sarah McLachlan's song *Full of Grace*.

+ *Tears from the Moon* was influenced by a song from Conjure One, also called *Tears from the Moon*.

+ *December* was influenced by Joshua Radin's song *Winter* and *A Memory Remains (Acoustic)*, a song by Narrow Skies.

+ The poem *Synchronicity of Loss* refers to and contains some lyrics to the song. *You Are My Sunshine*, author unknown but first copyrighted by Jimmy Davis and Charles Mitchell in 1940.

+ *Ever-Unfolding Rose* was first published in the poetry anthology *Glow: Self-Care Poetry For The Soul* By Indie Earth Publishing.

+ The poem *Éponine* is named after Éponine Thénardier, a character in Victor Hugo's 1862 novel *Les Misérables*. This poem was influenced by the song *Give Unto Me* by Evanescence.

+ The title for *Spiritual Flames* was selected to bridge together the concepts of romantic soulmates and twin flames.

- *The Dark Night of the Soul* references the spiritual crisis of the same name attributed to St. John of the Cross, a 16th-century Spanish poet and mystic.

- The title *Broken Hearts and Absent Gods* comes from a line in the song *Waste of Paint* by Bright Eyes.

- In *No Light*, the line "yet, as before Paul was Saul, I knowingly kick myself against the pricks" references the conversion story of the Apostle Paul. In addition, *No Light* also references Rumi, one the most notable philosophical and poetic minds in the recorded history of humanity. The quote referenced is, "The wound is the place where the light enters you." I do not claim to have a comprehensive or multifaceted understanding of this specific work, as I am neither an expert on Rumi and his works nor on the ethnolinguistic and sociocultural factors that shaped the Sufi experience. I reference him to cite his influence as part of this piece, as it is a stream-of-consciousness work.

- *As Time Turns the Page* is an abecedarian poem. According to the Poetry Foundation, an abecedarian follows the poetic structure or form in which the first letter of each line or stanza follows sequentially through the alphabet (starts at A and follows the sequence of the alphabet to end with Z).

- *Forever Hers* is a poem dedicated to Heavenly Mother, the Great Mother, the Queen of Heaven, the Feminine Divine.

- *Acrostic Sunrise* is an acrostic poem. According to the Poetry Foundation, an acrostic is a poetic structure or form in which the first letter of each line or stanza spells out a word, name, or phrase when read vertically.

✦ As in the introduction, *Lessons from Liminal Forces of Nature* references the iconic line "I am out with lanterns and looking for myself" by Emily Dickinson.

ACKNOWLEDGMENTS |

I extend my deepest gratitude and sincerest thanks to everyone who helped birth this book into reality and those sharing its message with the world.

- ✦ To my love, PWJ: Your unfailing love and unwavering support have helped me climb to the pinnacle of my hopes and give wings to my dreams, and there is no one else with whom I would want to watch them take flight.

- ✦ To my dear friend, Puppet/Poet: Your support, encouragement, and candid feedback on my writing have been instrumental in shaping me into the poet I am today. You will always be a source of inspiration and my unofficial poetry mentor.

- ✦ To my family: I love you more than you will ever know.

- ✦ To the poetry communities on Instagram and Poetizer: thank you so much for supporting me by reading my and commenting on my poetry. I am forever grateful for you.

- ✦ To you, dear Reader: Without you, my dreams would not be possible. Thank you for being a part of this healing journey with me. I hope you find the space waiting to be held for you within these words.

ABOUT THE AUTHOR |

A. W. Jones is a poet and writer residing in the Pacific Northwest. She made her literary debut in the poetry anthology, *Glow: Self-Care Poetry For The Soul*. A firm believer in the healing power of writing, *Mosaics of Shadow and Light* is her first poetry collection and a milestone in her journey of healing from complex childhood trauma. Jones graduated summa cum laude with a Bachelor of Arts in Psychology from California State University, Sacramento and is currently completing a Masters degree in Applied Behavior Analysis.

Connect with A. W. Jones
✦

Instagram: @awjonespoetry
Poetizer: @a redhead writes